Summary and Analysis

of

How To Do The Work: Recognize Your Patterns, Heal From Your Past + Create Yourself

By Dr. Nicole Lepera, The Holistic Psychologist Life Lessons

Note to Readers:

This is an unofficial summary & analysis of Dr. Nicole LePera's 'How to do the work: Recognize your Patterns, Heal from your past + Create Yourself' designed to enrich your reading experience.

whether directly or indirectly, of any advice or information presented, whether for breach of contract, tort, negligence, personal injury, criminal intent, or under any other cause of action.

You agree to accept all risks of using the information presented inside this book.

You agree that by continuing to read this book, where appropriate and/or necessary, you shall consult a professional (including but not limited to your doctor, attorney, or financial advisor, or such other advisor as needed) before using any of the suggested remedies, techniques, or information in this book.

Download Your Free Gift

Before you go any further, why not pick up a free gift from me to you?

Smarter Brain – a 10-part video training series to help you develop higher IQ, memory, and creativity – FAST!

Click here to get it before it expires!

Table of Contents

Preface

Dr. Nicole LePera's book 'How to Do the Work' is the pursuit of insight into the self and our place in the community. She writes the book intending to provide readers with tools to understand and harness the complex interconnectedness of their mind, body, and soul. All of us carry some unresolved trauma in our lives, and it finds a way to grow within our bodies and minds, weighing us down. Like most of us, Nicole found herself trying to move past her issues by doing the mundane things: cleaning the kitchen or walking the dog. But try as one may, it isn't easy to distract oneself from unresolved feelings.

A disconnect from the mind, body, and soul can manifest as sickness. If we can learn to be consciously aware of our thought patterns and habits, we can change the genes we were born with. Upon self-reflection, Nicole realized how her childhood experiences had profound effects on her spiritual self. As she delved deeper, she started applying her experiences to the knowledge she was building on integrating the whole person. Over time, she learned how to meet her inner child, examine the trauma bonds, set boundaries, and deal with the world with heightened emotional maturity. This understanding of mind-body-soul wellness is the heart of Holistic Psychology.

She often presents scientific data to corroborate her findings on one's emotions and their effects on the human body. At the end of the chapters, she has included a 'Do the work' section for readers to assess what they've learned and how they can apply what they've learned to aid in their SelfHealing. Along with that, she has also incorporated a 'Future Self Journal' (FSJ) section that provides prompts for readers to start journaling their feelings and work on themselves. Both of these sections have been included in the summary.

She has included a few anecdotes about her clients and her personal experiences in the book to further elaborate on the topic at hand. Some of these anecdotes have not made it to the summary, but the points she wishes to make have been included. Awakenings are not mystical experiences reserved only for monks, mystics, and poets. Anyone who wishes to break the cycle and craves change can find miracles to heal, thrive and shine. Nicole hopes to let the readers know that she is living proof of this truth with her book.

Introduction

The book 'How to Do the Work' is a testament to a revolutionary approach to mental, physical, and spiritual wellness called Holistic Psychology. Nicole explains this movement of empowerment as one that is committed to the daily practice of creating one's wellness by breaking negative patterns, healing from the past, and creating the conscious Self.

Holistic Psychology focuses on the mind, body, and soul in the service of rebalancing the body and nervous system and healing unresolved emotional wounds. By tapping into one's core, Holistic Psychology is able to get to the root of chronic pain, stress, fatigue, anxiety, gut dysregulation, and nervous system imbalance. It offers practical tools that enable practitioners to create new habits for themselves and understand the behavior of others. Nicole assures readers if they commit to doing the work every day, they will soon be looking in the mirror and feeling awestruck by the person looking back at them.

Healing is a conscious process that can be lived daily through changes in habits and patterns. Holistic methods are effective in helping one heal since the body, mind, and soul are connected. They harness the power of the physical with breathwork and bodywork, the psychological by changing one's relationship to their thoughts and past experiences, and the spiritual by connecting to the authentic Self. With Holistic Psychology, one can learn to reconnect to the inner guidance system. Every one of us has a built-in intuitive voice that is the voice of reasoning but is often ignored. This can be brought to light again by practicing Holistic Psychology.

Nicole wishes readers to take the book as an integrated approach to healing. Her intentions are not to bring down conventional psychotherapy. Instead, she hopes to propose an approach that embraces aspects of various modalities ranging from psychology to mindfulness to cultivate integrative techniques for wellness. She also asks readers to choose what resonates with them and let go of what doesn't. The practice of Holistic Psychology is rooted in freedom, choice, and empowerment.

Self-healing is an act that one must learn to do themselves to unleash their inner trauma and heal from them. The book offers readers self-directed learning models that can enable them to do the work of healing themselves every day. Deep change is only possible with a proper comprehension of the past and learning from it.

There are three parts to the book. The first part teaches readers how to build a foundation to become aware of the conscious Self. The second part explores the workings of the conscious and subconscious mind. In the third part, the author shows readers how they can use the knowledge they've gained from the first two parts and apply it in their real lives to manifest real change. As with all change, the road to creating an authentic self is not easy and requires time and patience. There are no quick fixes to empowerment and transformation, but those who can commit to going down the road will have one of the most profound experiences of their lives.

Nicole explains that when the reader is on their path of self-healing, they may feel the urge to quit when it gets too hard. At this point, she urges them to keep committed to the end goal and repeating the practice until it becomes a discipline. The first step to healing is to imagine a future that looks different from the present. When a person can envision an alternative to the reality in which they're living, they are ready to move forward.

Goal:

Part 0 of How to do the work by Dr. Nicole Lepera is dedicated to understanding how holistic psychology can positively influence our lives. Holistic Psychology is a movement of empowerment committed to creating our own wellness by breaking negative patterns, healing from our pasts, and creating our conscious self. By working with these holistic methods every day, we can harness the physical, psychological, and spiritual power because the body, mind, and soul are connected. The practice of Holistic Psychology is rooted in freedom, choice, and empowerment.

Lesson:

Activity 1:
A disconnect from the mind, body, and soul can manifest as sickness. Have you ever felt sick but never understood why you felt the way you did? Do you often find yourself unable to keep promises to yourself, attempting to make new choices or create new habits but always falling back on your old ones? Do you often find yourself feeling overwhelmed or unable to cope with stress?

Activity 2:
Self-healing is an act that one must learn to do themselves to unleash their inner trauma and heal from them. Have you taken the time to understand how you are feeling and why you may be feeling that way? Do you understand that the path to healing can be rough and broken at times, and do you have what it takes to keep going on, no matter what?

Activity 3:
Part 0 is dedicated to finding our conscious Self. Can you push yourself, not only towards being a better version of yourself but towards meeting your inner child? Are you ready to start the reparenting process and removing the trauma?

Checklist:

Key takeaways from Part 0 are:
- Healing is a daily commitment to doing the work.
- Holistic tools are practical and approachable. Change can feel overwhelming, but with consistency, it can be maintained.
- Western medicine is constrained by the belief that the mind and body are separate entities. Indigenous and Eastern cultures, on the other hand, honor the connections among the mind, body, and soul.
- Self-awareness can help reveal many of the previously hidden forces that manipulate and hold us back.

Action Plan:

- Start a Future Self Journal, a daily habit that encompasses every change you wish to make to your life.
- Start to imagine a future that looks different from the present.
- Witness the ways we remain stuck in our ways and what situations bring us there.

You Are Your Own Best Healer

In this chapter, Nicole talks about her clinical experiences, her learnings of CBT theory, and her realization that genetics do not bind people. As a clinical psychologist, most clients have come to her seeking help from being 'stuck.' Most of us find ourselves unable to change our past habits or create new routines to overcome old ones.

Nicole opens up about her dysfunctional family in which her mother struggled with phantom pains, and no one talked openly about their emotional turmoil. Nicole often wondered why people did what they did, which led her to get her Ph.D. in clinical psychology. However, she realized that the CBT model could be a bit rigid when applied in the real world.

As such, she was drawn to interpersonal therapy, an open-ended therapeutic model that uses the bond between client and practitioner. How we show up in our relationships is a mirror of our general wellness. Interpersonal therapy allows clients to engage in a healthy dynamic with a therapist that helps their healing. Theories on psychodynamic approaches suggest that people are driven by forces inside them.

Mind-Body-Soul Connection

The traditional model of mental health care can have its limitations. Western medicine is constrained by the belief that the mind and body are separate entities. Indigenous and Eastern cultures, on the other hand, honor the connections among the mind, body, and soul. When a person gets symptoms in their body, a physician helps provide them with medications, silencing the signs that our body is sending us. Mental health practitioners often ask their patients for their family history and prescribe antidepressants. When a patient is given a diagnosis, it decreases the incentive to change or explore root causes.

Genetic determinism proposes that our genes are determined at birth. However, emerging science dictates that the genes we inherit aren't fixed. We can make conscious choices about sleep, nutrition, relationships, and exercise to alter gene expression. The science of epigenetics proposes that we can become active participants in our well-being.

The Placebo Effect

Nicole has often been fascinated by the power of belief and the placebo effect, a term that describes the power of an inert substance (such as a sugar pill) to improve symptoms of illness. The mind can create fundamental changes in the body, and many cases of healing have been documented, ranging from Parkinson's disease to irritable bowel syndrome. When our body expects to get better, it sends out messages to start the healing process.

Similarly, the nocebo effect, the opposite of the placebo effect, exists in which our thoughts make us worse. Researchers would tell their participants that the inert drugs they're taking have severe side effects. Most people began to experience the warned-about side effects.

Holistic Psychology

Nicole was inspired to keep studying as much as she could about full-body healing after gaining insight into the mental and physical health connection. She formed the tenants of Holistic Psychology, which are as follows:

1. Healing is a daily commitment to doing the work.
2. Although many things are beyond our control, others are within our control. *God is in control*
3. Holistic tools are practical and approachable. Change can feel overwhelming, but with consistency, it can be maintained.

Nicole asks readers to spend some time reflecting on the following questions about being stuck.

- Do you often find yourself unable to keep promises to yourself, attempting to make new choices or create new habits but always falling back on your old ones? Yes
- Do you often find yourself reacting emotionally to events, feeling out of control, and even ashamed about your behaviors after the fact? Yes in past now notso much
- Do you often find yourself distracted or disconnected from yourself and others or from the present moment itself? Yes
- Do you often find yourself feeling overwhelmed and torn down by internal critical thoughts, making it difficult to tune in to your physical, emotional, and spiritual needs? Yes in past now notsomuch.

If you have answered 'yes' to one or more of these questions, the author proposes that you may be feeling stuck due to your past experiences and conditioning. The first way to create change is to practice imagining a different future.

Future Self Journal

Neethernther-

In the presence of God.

Future Self Journaling (FSJ) is a daily practice aimed at helping people break out of their subconscious autopilot. We can do so by consistently engaging in the following activities:

1. Witnessing the ways we remain 'stuck.'
2. Setting a conscious daily intention to change.
3. Setting small, actional steps to support daily choices aligned with the different future outcomes.
4. Empowering these daily choices despite the presence of mental resistance.

As readers sit with a pen and notepad, they are ready to begin the practice of making and keeping a small daily promise to themselves to create change.

The Conscious Self: Becoming Aware

Nicole talks about the conscious Self, finding oneself, and ways that we can look within ourselves in this chapter. She expounds that many of us don't have a real connection to who we are, but we constantly want to be better versions of ourselves. Most times, though, we fail to do so because we don't understand our minds and bodies. Most of her clients want to dive right in and meet their inner child, start the reparenting process and remove the trauma. Every one of us is searching for a quick fix, but we first need to gain the ability to witness our inner world.

Her own experience with consciousness and its awareness was brought about by a sign that read, "We do not remember days, we remember moments." Consciousness is more than being awake; it is a state of open awareness that allows us to witness ourselves and the life around us. Humans can practice sophisticated reasoning and complex multitasking. We can also think about thought, a process called metacognition. Nicole explains that we 'practice' thoughts all day long. But we must remember that we are not our thoughts. As we grow older, we fall under the influence of others and get disconnected from intuition.

present of God.

negative thoughts not from God.

21

The Conscious Self and The Subconscious Self

Self-awareness can help reveal many of the previously hidden forces that manipulate and hold us back. Most of us run our lives on autopilot. How we think, speak, and respond comes from the subconscious part of ourselves that has been conditioned by thoughts, patterns, and beliefs that are ingrained in our childhoods through a process called conditioning. Brain scans show that we operate only 5 percent of the day in the conscious state.

Humans are not evolutionarily wired for change, and whenever we try to do so, we face resistance from our minds and body. This is called the homeostatic impulse, a physiological function that regulates breathing to our heartbeat. The subconscious loves existing in a comfort zone. When we choose to leave our default programming, our subconscious mind attempts to pull us back to the familiar by creating mental resistance.

For many people, physical movement helps hone the attention muscle that is key to consciousness. One of her clients, Jessica, who suffered from anxiety and uncertainty, took up Yoga, which helped transform her mind. The attentional control she developed with her yoga practice helped her begin to take a second before reacting. Every one of us can change our brains at the physical level, a process called neuroplasticity. or allen

Goa to change + transform
Spiritual component

The Power of Belief

What we choose to believe can influence us in many ways. Nicole proposes that readers stop fixating on their negative thoughts and witness the body's sensations when feeling threatened. The best way to learn is to spend time alone, sit still, and hear the intuition. Our minds are powerful tools, and if we do not become consciously aware of the disconnection between our authentic Selves and our thoughts, we give our thoughts too much control in our daily lives. *silence.*

God

The author urges readers to try a few exercises to access their consciousness. To effect change, readers will need to create a routine to stick to. Here's how she proposes one build consciousness:

1. Find one to two minutes every day to practice being focused on and truly present in whatever you are doing. Whether you're doing the dishes or taking a bath, say to yourself, I am in this present moment.
2. Ground yourself at the moment. Our senses allow us to leave the monkey mind and find a deeper connection to the present moment. *God .*
3. After practicing this for one to two minutes, acknowledge that you gave yourself this time. *Be thankful Grateful to God*

FSJ: Consciousness Building

Nicole shares her Future Self Journaling prompts she used every day to create new habits in her daily life. She wrote these statements to serve as a constant reminder of her intention to change.

- Today, I am practicing being conscious of myself and my daily patterns.
- I am grateful for an opportunity to create change in my life.
- Today, I am conscious and aware whenever I choose.

She also advises people to set a reminder on their phones for random times throughout the day to practice consciousness.

A New Theory of Trauma

Trauma is the result of a profoundly catastrophic event, like abuse or neglect. The Centers for Disease Control and Prevention provides a scale called the Adverse Childhood Experiences (ACEs) to assess the level of trauma in people. But the ACE scales fail to register the range of emotional and spiritual traumas that people often go through. Traumatic experiences aren't always apparent, and the perception of trauma is just as valid as the trauma. In childhood, we are most likely to be traumatized when we consistently betray ourselves for love or are treated in ways that make us feel unworthy or unacceptable.

A loving parental relationship provides a secure base for a child to return to as they venture out into life. However, some parent figures who cannot deal with their emotional incapabilities project their unresolved traumas onto their children. Identifying the wounds is a fundamental step on the healing journey. The first step to healing is awareness.

The Archetypes of Childhood Trauma

Having a parent who denies your reality
Some parents ask their children to let go of their intuition and 'gut feeling' and listen to them instead. When a child comes to their parent looking for validation of their feelings, and the parent figure brushes their feelings away as inconsequential, they are taught that their perception of reality and related emotional experiences are not trustworthy.

Having a parent who does not see or hear you
Not being seen or heard in childhood is an experience of feeling emotionally disconnected from a parent figure. When a parent is running on autopilot, they cannot see their child, which prevents a deeper emotional connection with their child.

Having a parent who vicariously lives through you or molds you.
A 'stage parent' pushes their child to become an actress or a singer to full their own needs for fame, achievement, or attention. These children feel a burden to live up to their parents' expectations. Upon growing up, such children often cope with the misalignment of their careers, use substances, experience mental health issues, and even commit suicide.

Having a parent who does not model boundaries
Children instinctively understand boundaries. Instances in which parents violate their boundaries by reading their diaries can teach them that loved ones can cross boundaries. Such children may become highly secretive and protective of their personal details. In contrast, they may believe crossing boundaries are part of 'closeness' and 'love.'

Having a parent who is overly focused on appearance

Parents may project their need for validation onto their children, obsessing about their presentation and looks. Children learn that some parts of their physical appearance are 'acceptable' and some are not. It is also projected on them when parents act a certain way at home and something else outside, teaching them that humans have 'pseudo selves.'

Having a parent who cannot regulate their emotions
Most of us did not have parents who were able to identify and regulate our feelings. Some parents scream, slam doors, throw things, or storm off when dealing with an emotional outburst. Others use silent treatment and withdraw love from their child. When parent-figures shut down, we experience an overall lack of emotional regulation and do not develop coping skills to build emotional resilience.

Coping with Trauma

Lazarus and Folkman outlined adaptive and maladaptive coping strategies. Adaptive coping is an action we take to help us return to feelings of safety, such as facing a problem head-on or redirecting negative thoughts. Maladaptive coping strategies include trying to please people, bursting with anger, and disassociation. Such coping strategies prevent us from reliving our past trauma. However, when our needs are consistently unmet, our pain and disconnection are compounded. We all carry unresolved trauma. The first step towards healing in mind and body is knowing what we're dealing with.

Do The Work: Identify Your Childhood Wounds

Nicole advises readers to take some time to reflect and write about their unresolved trauma. They may use journal prompts such as:

In my childhood, when my parent-figure(s) _____, I felt _____

To cope, I _____

Trauma Body

The scientific data helps corroborate her findings on the human body and stress. Every client who arrives at her office experiencing psychological symptoms also suffers from underlying physical health issues. Unresolved trauma can weave itself into the fabric of our being. They make us more likely to develop a host of physical and psychological conditions ranging from depression and anxiety to heart attacks, cancer, obesity, and stroke.

Stress is an internal condition that challenges homeostasis, the state of physical, emotional, and mental balance. When we are stressed, the body shifts its resources from maintaining homeostasis, that happy place of well-being and balance, to protecting itself. As an adaptive response, we can develop coping strategies to help return us to our psychological and physiological baseline by:

- Seeking supportive resources.
- Learning how to self-soothe.
- Assisting our nervous systems to return to homeostasis.

This process of leaving and then returning to our baseline of balance is called allostasis.

The body's stress response is often referred to as a fight-or-flight mechanism. When the body perceives a threat, it sends a message to the rest of the body, prompting the various systems to mobilize themselves to help us survive. Once our immune system gets the signal that we're living in a near-constant threat state, it repeatedly sends out chemicals that cause inflammation throughout the body. These chemicals act as a kind of fire starter for a wide array of symptoms of imbalance and dysfunction, increasing our risk of developing autoimmune diseases, chronic pain, and other illnesses ranging from heart disease to cancer. If left immobilized or stuck in this response, our immune system will continue to activate a full-body inflammatory reaction.

Polyvagal Theory

The Polyvagal Theory was proposed by Dr. Stephen Porges, which offers insight into trauma and the body's stress response. The term polyvagal refers to the vagus nerve, which connects the brain and the gut. The location and function of these nerves help us understand why the body reacts so swiftly when we're stressed: why our hearts race when we run into an ex or why feelings of panic make us feel short of breath. When we are in a state of homeostasis, the vagus nerve acts as a neutral break, keeping us calm and open, helping us be our most social selves.

In activation mode, the vagus nerve sends SOS signals to the nervous system, making our hearts pump harder, activating stress responses that increase cortisol levels and body temperature. In this heightened state, pain doesn't register, we lose our sense of smell, shoulders hunch, and the voice takes a stressed-out tone. Patients who deal with chronic stress state complain of:

- Lack of emotional resilience
- Inability to form meaningful connections
- Issues with concentration
- Difficulty performing higher-functioning cognitive tasks, such as planning for the future
- Trouble delaying gratification

One of the most common stress responses is immobilization or' freezing.' Sometimes, our heart rate slows down, bowels clench up, and breathing may stop causing us to pass out due to chronic stress. This can happen when the body feels there is no hope for survival. This is disassociation mode. Here, people leave their bodies psychologically and are detached from everything else. Such people often complain of not being able to connect with anyone or cultivate emotional depth.

Co-regulation

When we feel safe, it is reflected in our eyes, voice, and body language. Our energies are transferable with other people. This is why we feel better and calmer around certain people because our nervous systems respond to theirs. The ability to co-regulate is established in childhood. One of the most critical behaviors we learn from our loved ones is applying internal coping strategies that help return us to the safe and creative space of social mobilization during times of stress.

Children who grew in a chaotic house cannot freely return to the safe social engagement mode. They were taught to internalize the state and generalize that the world is a scary place. Some people thrive on watching the news or being in a relationship with an unstable partner because this is the only thing that makes them feel like they did when they were a child. The uncertainty brings a rush of anger and disgust.

Do The Work: Assess Your Nervous System Dysregulation

Nicole asks readers to witness themselves and their feelings when under stress. When feeling under pressure, she proposes the following steps to help restore balance in the nervous system:

1. Find a smell, taste, or a visual in the current environment and focus your full attention.
2. Close your eyes and take a deep breath. Repeat the words, I am safe, and I am at peace.
3. Be mindful of what information you are consuming.
4. Go outside and experience any aspect of the natural environment.

FSJ: Restoring Balance

Nicole wrote the following prompts in her journal on her SelfHealing process. She urges the readers to do the same:

- Today I am practicing restoring balance to my nervous system.
- I am grateful for an opportunity to create calm in my life.
- Today, I am bringing one moment of much-needed calm to my body.
- Change in this area allows me to feel more peace.

Mind-Body Healing Practices

This chapter explores how we can start the mind-body healing practices and bring positive change in our lives. Nicole speaks about her client, Ally, who could get herself out of the self-blame game by listening to her body. She did so by starting to note her body's responses to her emotions and held space for them without judgment or reproach. Healing begins with learning how to tap into our body's needs and reconnect with our intuitive Self. Even though our nervous system reactions are automatic, there are ways to improve the vagal tone and return more quickly to the safe space of social engagement mode.

Nicole then proposes several processes that can help readers get started on their healing journey. The brain-to-body conversation is called a top-down process. The top-down processes recruit our brain to guide our body on a path toward healing. An example is meditation, in which by training one's attention, people regulate their autonomic nervous system responses. Such top-down practices can help activate, challenge, and tone the vagus nerve to build tolerance. When we can push ourselves within safe confines, it prepares us to deal with stresses outside our control.

The chronic and overwhelming stress we experience in childhood can make it harder for our bodies to rest and digest properly. Our guts are made of the enteric nervous system (ENS) that communicates with the rest of the body. Chronic and overwhelming stress in childhood can make it harder for our bodies to rest and digest properly. Nicole proposes that the quickest way to improve gut health is to eat whole, nutrient-dense food. The direct line between the gut and the brain makes each meal an opportunity for healing and nourishment. She also advises readers to take up intermittent fasting, a process of depriving the body of food for over 12 to 18 hours. Studies have shown that intermittent fasting increases mental understanding, learning, and alertness as well.

Most people who deal with stress also complain of not getting enough sleep. Sleep deprivation is linked to depression, cardiovascular illness, and even cancer, obesity, and neurological conditions, such as Alzheimer's disease. The most important way to improve sleep is to help ease the parasympathetic system into its happy place of relaxation. Maintaining a consistent bedtime routine allows the body to enter into a parasympathetic state. Taking a bath, snuggling with a pet, or talking to your partner can promote a sense of calm.

We cannot control the autonomic nervous system, but we can control how we breathe, thereby decreasing our heart rate, and calming our minds. Breathwork engages the vagus nerve, communicating to the brain that we are in a non-threatening environment. Nicole proposes inhaling through the nose, holding the breath, and exhaling to challenge and expand the lungs.

Healing with Movement

Yoga helps activate the vagus nerve and engages both the mind and body. It can test our physical limits, further stressing our system and offering an opportunity to reconnect with the calming power of our breath. As we take on more taxing postures, our vagus nerve learns how to control our stress response and return more readily to the state of calmness and safety where healing happens.

Healing with Play

As adults, we can still experience similar joyous freedom when we allow ourselves to play. This might involve dancing, playing music, singing, or dressing up, and entering an imaginary world. When we lose ourselves in this way, we can sometimes enter a flow state of pure enjoyment.

Every day in the journal, writing similar versions of the following statements can remind one's intention to change, make new choices, and create a new habit.

- Today I am practicing using a deep belly breath to help calm my body and bring me a sense of safety and peace.
- I am grateful for the opportunity to learn a new way to regulate my body.
- Today, I am calm and grounded in my body.
- Change in this area allows me to feel better able to tolerate stress.

Goal:

The first part of How to do the work by Dr. Nicole Lepera teaches readers to identify with themselves and learn about their behaviors, trauma, and experiences. Humans are not evolutionarily wired for change, and whenever we try to do so, we face resistance from our minds and body. Still, by consciously being aware of our bodies, we can create positive change. This part aims to educate readers about the various kinds of childhood trauma and how we can learn to cope with trauma. It also teaches us about the polyvagal nerve and how to work with the muscle to keep us calm and open.

Lesson:

Activity 1:
While activated, the vagus nerve sends SOS signals to the nervous system, making our hearts pump harder, activating stress responses that increase cortisol levels. Do you feel a lack of emotional resilience? Are you unable to form meaningful connections? Do you have issues with concentration? Do you have trouble delaying gratification?

Activity 2:
. In childhood, we are most likely to be traumatized when we consistently betray ourselves for love or are treated in ways that make us feel unworthy or unacceptable. What archetype of childhood trauma do you identify yourself with? Can you perform adaptive coping, an action to help you return to feelings of safety, or do you find yourself stuck with maladaptive coping strategies such as bursting with anger and disassociation?

Activity 3:

We can start the mind-body healing practices by noting our body's responses to the emotions and learning to tap into our body's needs. What needs are showing in your body today? Have you taken the time to heal your mind and body with play and movement?

Checklist:

Key takeaways from Part 1 are:
- The best way to learn about our feelings and emotions is to spend time alone, sit still, and hear intuition.
- Some parent figures who cannot deal with their emotional incapability project their unresolved traumas onto their children.
- Even though our nervous system reactions are automatic, there are ways to improve the vagal tone and return more quickly to the safe space of social engagement mode.
- For many people, physical movement such as running or Yoga helps hone the attention muscle that is key to consciousness.

Action Plan:

- Practice consciousness and be aware of your daily actions.
- Witness your feelings under stress and be aware of how you deal with trauma.
- Start the mind and body healing process with physical activities such as Yoga or dancing, or start playing music or singing to enter a state of pure enjoyment.

The Power of Belief

As children, we are limited by what we can cognitively and emotionally understand based on our developmental age. Given these limitations, we may believe that we are bad when a parent figure raises a hand to us instead of knowing that this person has difficulty managing their anger. Sometimes our reality is too painful to understand, so we make up an alternative story that guides us through the darkness.

Nicole talks about her childhood and instances where she believed herself to be unimportant because her mother wasn't emotionally available to her needs. Beliefs about ourselves are filters that are placed over the lens of how we view our world. The more we practice specific thoughts, the more our brain wires itself to default to these thought patterns. The habit of thinking about a particular idea over and over again changes our brain, making it easier to default to such thought patterns in the future.

When a belief is repeatedly validated, it can become what is called a core belief. Once a core belief is formed, information that does not conform to our beliefs is discarded. We subconsciously filter information to help sort out our environment, which is done by the reticular activating system (RAS). The brain can sometimes use the RAS filter as a defense mechanism. An idealized view of our childhood becomes a core belief that may come from self-preservation. In real life, no childhood is perfect. Allowing ourselves to witness the entirety of our past honestly and current experiences are fundamental to our healing.

We learn a language, movement, and social interaction during our infancy. Since we are most vulnerable and dependent at this stage, the most significant imprinting comes from our parent figures. We look to them for clues about connecting, navigating the world, and coping with stress, which is called co-regulation. When we aren't taught how to regulate our emotions, we are stuck in a fight-flight mode and devote our resources to manage stress.

Childhood Interrupted

As our brains develop, our needs expand from the basics of shelter, food, and love. Spiritually, our individual souls have three basic needs:

1. To be seen
2. To be heard
3. To uniquely express our most authentic Self.

Few people, let alone stressed parents, have the tools to meet all of these needs all of the time. When children's emotional needs are not adequately met, they often develop a subconscious core belief that they are not worthy of having these needs met. An overwhelmed parent figure may be unable to deal with children's emotions and label them as too sensitive. Nicole explains that she sees this in many of her male clients who were discouraged from expressing emotion.

The external environment, such as our educational systems, shapes our core beliefs as well. In adulthood, we tend to see the world through the filters applied by the core beliefs. Continuing to strengthen these core beliefs can increase disconnection from our authentic Selves. The more disconnected we are, the more depressed, lost, confused, stuck, and hopeless we feel.

Nicole expounds that our beliefs are compelling and continue to shape our daily experiences. These beliefs were not formed overnight and will not change overnight. With dedication and persistence, we can change them.

Do the Work: Do a Core Beliefs Inventory

Nicole urges readers to take some time to reflect on and journal their core beliefs. We hold core beliefs about ourselves and the world around us. She offers the following journal prompts to help readers reflect.

While witnessing my thoughts throughout the day, I am noticing themes:

1. About myself:
2. About others or my relationships:
3. About my past:
4. About my present:
5. About my future:

FSJ: Creating a New Belief

With the knowledge that beliefs are practiced thoughts, we can learn to create a new belief by practicing a new thought. We can start by picking a belief and beginning to change it. For instance, the thought 'I am not good enough' may be changed with 'I am enough.'

It is best to make this new thought a daily affirmation. Readers may wish to write it in a journal every day or recite it several times a day.

Meet Your Inner Child

Our relationship with our primary parent figures is the foundation of the dynamics of all the relationships we have in adulthood. The attachment between mother and child is defined as a lasting psychological connectedness between human beings. A study studied different attachment styles by observing a child's response when the mother briefly left the child in a room.

1. **Secure:** A securely attached infant may get upset for a brief period after the mother leaves the room but will recover quickly.
2. **Anxious-resistant**: The anxious-resistant infant may be so stressed and distressed by the mother's absence that they remain upset the whole time the mother is gone. When she returns, the child isn't comforted easily, remains clingy, and may even punish the mother for leaving.
3. **Avoidant:** Children in this category show almost no stress response when the mother leaves and almost no reaction when the mother returns. These children do not seek out their mothers for comfort. Some actively avoid the mothers. This is typically a product of a disconnected parent-figure
4. **Disorganized-disoriented:** These children show no predictable pattern of response. Sometimes they are highly distressed and stressed; other times, they show no reaction at all.

The safer and more secure the bond between a child and their parent figures, the safer the child feels in the world. The inability to form secure attachments in childhood has been linked to social anxiety, conduct disorders, and other psychological diagnoses.

Introducing the Inner Child

Nicole talks about her childhood and how she practiced disengagement to distance herself from everything else. This disengagement began to show itself in her relationships as an adult. As she practiced self-witnessing, she began to notice her thoughts. Therapist John Bradshaw proposed that any of us end up in 'toxic' relationships because we never addressed the traumas that happened in childhood.

We all have a childlike part of ourselves filled with wonder and connection to the inner wisdom of our Self. It can be accessed only when we are safely in the social connection zone of our nervous system. When not acknowledged, the inner childlike part of us can run rampant in our adult life. Inner child wounds are the consistently unmet emotional, physical, and spiritual needs from our childhood expressed through our subconscious that continue to impact our present Self. The majority of us feel unheard and unloved and carry this pain with us throughout our lives.

Our romantic partners tend to activate our wounds at the most intense levels. Some of us argue loudly, slam doors, or leave in an argument. Many of us acct like children when we are upset because we are emotionally illiterate.

The seven inner child archetypes are as follows:

1. **The Caretaker:** Gains a sense of identity and self-worth through neglecting their own needs.
2. **The overachiever**: Uses external validation as a way to cope with low self-worth.

3. **The underachiever:** Keeps themselves small, unseen, and beneath their potential due to fear of criticism or shame about failure.
4. **The rescuer:** Views others as helpless, incapable, and dependent and derives their love and self-worth from being in a position of power.
5. **The life of the party:** This is the always happy and cheerful comedic person who never shows pain, weakness, or vulnerability.
6. **The yes-person.** Drops everything and neglects all needs in the service of others.
7. **The hero worshipper:** Believes that the only way to receive love is to reject their own needs and desires and view others as models to learn how to live.

One common defense against the pain of unmet childhood needs is an idealization. We dream that our lives would only change if someone would swoop in and save us. This is why some people put pressure on their romantic partners to fulfill their desires. Others think they will be 'saved' when they get a great job, buy a house, or have children. Once they've achieved their goals, they find themselves unhappy and unfulfilled again. The wounded inner child carries this powerlessness and hopes that others will change our circumstances. We choose the quick fix- drugs, alcohol, or sex to feel pleasure at the moment and dull our pain.

Meet Your Inner Child

Nicole explains that what we're doing, feeling, and thinking every day is a living replica of past experiences in one way or another. She urges readers to look back at the past with the maturity of an adult brain to put things into proper perspective. Accepting that we have an inner child with wounds will help remove disappointment in our inability to change the feeling of being 'stuck.' When we begin to start honoring what the inner child is telling us, we can become present and aware. The greater the presence and awareness grow, the greater our ability to distinguish between our inner child reactions and our authentic Self.

Do The Work: Write An Inner Child Letter To Yourself

Spend some time reflecting and witnessing your inner child through the day, and note which of your inner child archetypes are most frequently activated. Write a letter letting yourself know that the inner child does not have to feel or be that way anymore. End the letter with:
I see you, I hear you, and I love you always.
Wise Adult (Insert Your Name)

Readers who are interested in a guided inner child meditation can visit the website: https://yourholisticpsychologist.com.

Ego Stories

Despite its pronounced impact on our lives, most of us have no awareness of the ego and how it drives our behavior. The ego is our sense of self, our personal identity, and our self-worth. It is formed through the beliefs and ideas imparted to us by our parent figures, friends, immediate community, and environment. Rigidity is part of the ego's defensive stance as its job is to protect the vulnerable inner child. When our opinions are questioned, the ego believes that our core self is being threatened.

If we do not practice witnessing the ego, it will fight to assert itself and dominate, leading to insecurity and low self-worth. In its reactive state, the ego can make us want to defend, condemn, win and have the last word. The ego puts up barriers to make sure we're never hurt because, in every opportunity for positive change, there is also the chance of the pain of failure.

Ego Activation

Ego stories can take on a life-or-death quality. When someone disagrees with a person, their opinions don't feel limited to a specific topic but end up being about who they are. Often when disagreement does occur, the goal is not to try to get closer to a shared truth. Instead, it invalidates each other's realities and destroys the other person to establish your worth and power.

As children, we are taught that to appear acceptable, we have to maintain our connections. When we consistently repress any part of our authentic self to receive love, and the act of repression becomes an ego story. The more we deny parts of our shadow self, the more shame we feel and the more disconnected we become from our intuition.

When we don't know why a person is behaving in a way that makes us upset, our ego goes into hyperdrive to try to figure out why by insisting that we would never do something so terrible. This is why judging others is so addictive; it relieves us from the ego's internal struggle with shame.

How To Do The Work With Your Ego

The work begins by simply witnessing. When we exist on autopilot, our ego holds the reins, so actively engaging the conscious mind helps loosen our ego's hold on our daily existence. Once we become aware and conscious, we can view our ego's thought patterns and fears without judgment.

Step one: Allow the ego to introduce itself by seeing it as a separate entity from you.
Step two: Have a friendly encounter with your ego by noticing how often you speak about yourself.
Step three: Name your ego. It is a powerful act of separating yourself from it.
Step four: Meet the activated ego. Understand that you are not your thoughts.

As we navigate the ego in a more empowered way, we can have difficult conversations without feeling threatened when questioned or challenged. The more we practice this awareness, the more our ego softens.

The Concept of Self-truth

As we build up attentional controls and practice self-witnessing, we are forced to start looking more objectively at our behaviors. Our shadow self consists of all the unsavory parts of ourselves, our relationships, our past, and our parent figures that we are ashamed of. Our projections, or our internal emotions that we externalize onto others, are messages from our shadow Self.

Living unconsciously and unaware of our thoughts, patterns, and behaviors, we are wholly identified with our egoic concept of who we are. Our automatic response is to externalize uncomfortable feelings, blaming everyone else. This state is the ego consciousness. The ultimate goal, however, is to cultivate empowerment consciousness, an acceptance of the ego. \

Do The Work: Meet Your Shadow

Take some time reflecting and writing using these prompts:

- When you feel jealousy, ask yourself: What do I feel the other person has that I feel I am lacking?
- How often do you give others advice, and why do you give it?
- How do you speak about yourself to others?
- How do you speak about others when they are not around?

Anytime our ego is threatened, we can become emotionally reactive, throwing tantrums or detaching. These responses are stored deep in our subconscious and cannot be changed immediately. As we begin to be more aware of the ego, we may feel the compulsive need to react in an old way. It's important to remember that it is okay to do so.

FSJ: Changing Ego Consciousness To Empowerment Consciousness

Nicole urges readers to create a space before returning to older ego reactions. Here are some journal prompts that can help.

- Today I am practicing breaking old habits of emotional reactivity.
- I am grateful for the opportunity to choose new responses to my daily life.
- Today I am calm and grounded in presence.
- Change in this area allows me to feel more in control of my choices.
- Today I am practicing when I use my breath to ground my reactions and make space for new, conscious choices.

Trauma Bonds

Our dependency on other people to survive and thrive doesn't end in childhood; as adults, we continue to seek out attachments, primarily through romantic relationships. The results of research by Dr. Hazan and Dr. Shaver found that childhood attachment provides the basis for romantic relationships in adulthood. Typically, if a person had distant, erratic, or abusive relationships in childhood, they will seek out the same kind of bonds in adulthood.

Dr. Patrick Carnes coined the term 'traumatic bonding' to describe the relationship between two people with insecure attachment. By his definition, we enter into a traumatic bond when we seek comfort from the source of our trauma—in this case, the person who abuses or hurts us. A trauma bond is a relationship pattern that keeps us stuck in dynamics that do not support our authentic Self's expression.

Common signs of a trauma bond are:
1. Having an obsessive, compulsive pull towards particular relationships even though you know the relationship will likely have problematic long-term consequences.
2. Your needs are rarely met in particular relationships, or you are unaware of what your needs are in any relationship.
3. You continue to betray yourself in particular relationships to get your needs met and lack self-trust.

Trauma bonds are the extensions of how we adapted in the absence of having an intrinsic need met. We use them to maintain an armor of self-protection so that our inner child wounds can never be opened again.

Shame, Addiction, and Trauma Bonds

Children born into environments filled with stress will seek similar environments as adults. We are always subconsciously seeking to relive our past because we are creatures of comfort. When the subconscious identifies stress responses, we may confuse signals of threat and stress for sexual attraction and chemistry. This is why issues often emerge after the sex-infused honeymoon period in the early phases of our romantic relationships. We often associate love with a trauma response because we feel numb without it. If there is peace, people initiate their own stress and feel ashamed about it later.

The shame emerges from the feeling that we should know better. When we are engaged in trauma bonding, we are pulled in by the subconscious wounds of our past. Trauma bonds are physical responses running through our bodies, working to keep us in the exact same place we're in.

Trauma Bond Archetypes

The first step in breaking trauma bond patterns is witnessing them.

1. **Having a parent who denies your reality:**
   Children who had parents who denied their feelings on growing up don't acknowledge their own needs. These people can be martyrs, the ones who act selflessly to their own detriment. They are typically conflict-avoidant and follow the mantra If you're okay, I'm okay.

2. **Having a parent who does not see or hear you:**
   People with such parents often feel they must quiet their true nature in order to receive love. Those who were subject to silent treatment often do the same to others when they're threatened.

3. **Having a parent who vicariously lives through you:**
   Such people often rely on external guidance from partners, friends, or mentors for input or feedback on their big and small decisions. Because they have always been told what they feel, they have no connection to intuitive guidance.

4. **Having a parent who does not model boundaries:**
   In adulthood, such people may find themselves overriding their own needs in relationships and consistently allowing their limits to be crossed. Over time this denial of need can morph into anger or resentment.

5. **Having a parent who is overly focused on appearance:**

Such children grow up into adults who constantly measure themselves against others to see if they measure up. This reliance on external appearance leads them to be focused on the image they present externally.

6. **Having a parent who cannot regulate their emotions:** Such adults often lack adaptive emotional coping skills and model the same emotional reactivity as their parents. Some explode, storm around the house, slamming doors, or engage in disassociation.

Nicole advises readers to write down the names of people they are closest to and explain how these relationships make them feel.

Authentic Love

Just because we are in a trauma bond doesn't necessarily mean that the relationship is doomed. These bonds are teachers that teach us what areas need working on. Nicole shares her relationship insights with her partner, Lolly, and how they put the work into bettering themselves to better the relationship. When two people allow each other the freedom and support to be fully seen, heard, and Self-expressed, authentic love is formed. It feels safe and is rooted in the awareness that the other person is not property.

It doesn't always feel 'good' or romantic, and there may be times when you feel bored or unsettled. Like everything else, authentic love requires work.

Do The Work: Identify Your Trauma Bonds

Nicole urges readers to reflect upon how they feel and react when they perceive someone denying their thoughts, feelings, or experiences. They may do so by using the journal prompt:

Today, when (insert an experience) I feel _____ and I react by

_____

Boundaries

Boundaries protect us and help us connect to our intuitive Self. They provide a necessary limit for every relationship and, most importantly, the one we have with ourselves. When boundaries are in place, we feel safer expressing our authentic wants and needs. But if we come from an enmeshed family dynamic in which parents are overly involved in their children's lives, we often put others first and play the martyr.

Most of us have never learned how to say 'no.' The first barrier to boundary work is the notion of 'niceness.' We constantly try to play nice such that others will like us. But the reality is being 'not nice' enables us to assert our own value. It isn't about being mean, arrogant, or inconsiderate but knowing what we want. Learning to say no is often the kindest thing we can do for ourselves and those we love.

While some of us struggle with nonexistent boundaries, some create too-rigid boundaries and practice emotional withdrawal to stay separate from others. If a boundary was repeatedly violated in childhood by a primary attachment figure, we might continue to feel unsafe in most other relationships.

Nicole urges readers to take the time to witness different aspects of their lives and use this self-diagnostic tool to help identify where the boundaries fall.

Rigid:
- Has few intimate/close relationships
- Has a chronic fear of rejection
- Has difficulty asking for help
- Is fiercely private

Loose

- Engages in compulsive people-pleasing
- Defines self-worth by the opinions of others
- Has a general inability to say no
- Consistently overshares private information
- Is a chronic fixer/helper/saver/rescue

Flexible:

- Is aware of and values own thoughts, opinions, and beliefs
- Knows how to communicate needs to others
- Shares personal information appropriately
- Is consistently able to say no when needed and accepts others' doing the same
- Can regulate emotions, allowing others to express themselves

When our needs are not met, instead of pointing the finger at another person, it's better to ask ourselves: What do I need to do to make sure that my needs are better met?

Types of Boundaries

The first type of boundary is a physical boundary. Loose physical boundaries can make us see our worth in how we look, what our bodies can do, and how others view us. Honoring the body's wants and needs can look like outlining our personal space and describing our preferred level of physical contact.

The second type of boundary is a resource boundary. When we give too much of ourselves to others, even when we don't have the energy for it, we violate our resource boundaries. However, having a rigid resource boundary means adhering to a predetermined schedule every day and lacking flexibility.

Then there is the mental/ emotional boundary that is often crossed in families with enmeshment issues. When we have loose emotional boundaries, we feel responsible for the mental states around us and a need to keep everyone happy. There is often a complete lack of interest in anyone else's worldview in those of us with too-rigid mental boundaries. If we are stubborn and adamant about our own beliefs or emotions, we remain separate from the people around us, making genuine connection impossible.

Emotional Dumping and Oversharing

Some people become oversharers when their parents overshare too much information too soon. This causes people to become 'air fillers,' talking about themselves anytime they feel any discomfort. It is beneficial for us to put up boundaries around our internal world so we can decide to keep things private.

Another common outcome of mental boundarylessness is emotional dumping: spilling emotional issues onto a person without being empathetic to their emotional state. This is different from 'venting,' which revolves around one singular topic and helps with stress release. Emotional dumping involves the airing of negative, circular, and obsessive thoughts. People who are prone to emotional dumping are often caught in the loop of emotional addiction. Emotional dumpers feel comfortable only when discussing topics that allow them to feel depressed. When faced with the unfamiliar positive, they turn the conversation back to the more distressing baseline where their entire system feels at home.

How to Set Boundaries

The first step to setting boundaries is to examine our life and notice where boundaries are lacking. Nicole asks readers to witness how they feel after they've met someone. We are not in the thinking mind when we're witnessing how we feel; instead, we are noticing how something or someone registers in our body. Once we start noticing our bodily sensations, we can assess where our boundaries are lacking.

When the boundaries are assessed, we can determine how to practice setting them. We need to start communicating clearly about our boundaries to set us up for successful change. We could let the other person know why we're setting our boundaries to help them see. It is helpful to communicate a boundary at a time when both parties are emotionally settled. When we're activated, we're in no state to receive anything challenging. The discomfort we face while setting boundaries will save us years of anger and resentment.

The third step is to maintain the new boundary. Once we've set a boundary, it's vital to remain present and calm, resisting the urge to defend or overexplain. As we begin to practice the tools of SelfHealing, we begin to see others from a bird's-eye view. When we do so, we often find that compassion emerges for other people in our relationships, even those with whom we may have chosen to cut contact.

Do the Work: Create a New Boundary

Nicole urges readers to look closely at their relationships with their partners, parents, and work colleagues. It's best to determine overall comfort and choosing how close we let other people in. After identifying the required changes to help maintain a reasonable boundary, we could start making it a daily affirmation. Using these prompts may help:

- I don't feel comfortable when _____
- To make myself feel more comfortable, I _____

It is crucial to communicate the new boundary with others. Saying, "I am making some changes so that [insert your intention for your new boundary] and hope you can understand that this is important to me" may help communicate your boundary better.

Goal:

The second part of How to do the work by Dr. Nicole Lepera explores the workings of the conscious and subconscious mind. When a belief is repeatedly validated, it can become what is called a core belief. Once a core belief is formed, information that does not conform to our beliefs is discarded. We learn a language, movement, and social interaction from our parent figures, and when they cannot teach us how to regulate our emotions, we are stuck in a fight-flight mode. Our relationship with our primary parent figures is the foundation of the dynamics of all the relationships we have in adulthood. This part teaches readers to understand their relationship dynamics and set boundaries to navigate life better.

Lesson:

Activity 1:
Spiritually, our individual souls have three basic needs: to be seen, heard, and uniquely express our most authentic Self. Do you feel like your emotional needs are being met? Do you feel you are not worthy of your needs being met due to your parents' inability to fulfill your emotional needs as a child?

Activity 2:
As adults, we continue to seek out attachments to survive and thrive primarily through romantic relationships. Do you feel a compulsive pull towards a relationship even though you know it will have problematic long-term consequences? Do you feel that your needs are met in a relationship? Do you continue to betray yourself to get your needs met and lack self-trust?

Activity 3:
The first step to setting boundaries is to examine our life and notice where boundaries are lacking. Boundaries protect us and help us connect to our intuitive Self. Do you find it difficult to say 'no'? Do you always like to play nice even though deep down you know that it doesn't suit your needs or wants? Do you have rigorous boundaries wherein you struggle to let people in?

Checklist:

Key takeaways from Part 1 are:
- The more we practice specific thoughts, the more our brain wires itself to default to these thought patterns, so it is essential to filter out negativity and focus on the positives.
- The inability to form secure attachments in childhood has been linked to social anxiety, conduct disorders, and other psychological diagnoses.
- When boundaries are in place, we feel safer expressing our authentic wants and needs and can work towards a mutually beneficial relationship.
- For many people, physical movement such as running or Yoga helps hone the attention muscle that is key to consciousness.

Action Plan:

- Analyze your core beliefs: think about the relationship you have with yourself and others as well as your past, present, and future.
- Spend some time reflecting and witnessing your inner

child through the day, and note which of your inner child archetypes are most frequently activated.

- Analyze the type of boundaries you currently have in your relationships and learn to set them such that your needs are better met.

Reparenting

Awakenings aren't instantaneous but an accumulation of insights over time. They often emerge from a state of inner turmoil in a natural setting, and they connect us to some kind of spiritual practice. Awakening is a rebirth of the self that involves tearing down parts of who we were when we lived in an autopilot state of existence.

If we lived with an emotionally immature parent figure, our needs were likely routinely unmet or dismissed. An emotionally immature parent figure may throw tantrums, and often the whole family unit ends up revolving around their moods. Understand their lack of emotional maturity frees us from emotional loneliness as we realize that their negativity wasn't about us but about them. The way we move forward is to have the awareness that we can become wise parents to ourselves. This is a process called reparenting, and it enables us to relearn how to meet the unmet needs of our inner child.

When we reparent, we begin by learning how to identify our physical, emotional, and spiritual needs, and then we practice noticing the conditioned way we've gone about attempting to get those needs met. With the help of the wise inner parent, we can learn how to validate our reality and feelings by witnessing them rather than instinctually judging or ignoring them. It begins by trusting ourselves by setting small promises to ourselves to engage in daily acts of self-care.

The Four Pillars of Reparenting

The first pillar of reparenting is emotional regulation. Emotional regulation is our ability to cope with stress in a flexible, tolerant, and adaptive way.

The second pillar is loving discipline. We do this by making and keeping small promises and developing daily routines and habits.

The third pillar goes hand in hand with loving discipline: self-care. Self-care is the act of learning to identify and care for our physical and emotional wants and needs, especially those that were denied in childhood.

The fourth pillar, one of the ultimate goals of the work, is to rediscover our childlike sense of wonder. This state is made up of a combination of creativity and imagination, joy and spontaneity, and playfulness.

Dealing With Loneliness, Disappointment, and Anger

Reparenting is hard, consistent work that requires us to identify our evolving needs and coping strategies constantly. It's not just the judgment of outsiders that we will face but also the judgment that comes from within. Loneliness is a theme that comes up throughout the healing journey but especially during the reparenting process. We must remember that we cannot deeply engage with reparenting until we have become conscious of ourselves.

One realization many SelfHealers have while reparenting is that they've been living with unexpressed anger. Opening our eyes to how we were let down, rejected, or traumatized in our past can awaken latent feelings of anger and rage. Many SelfHealers go back to their parent figures and demand to be heard or ask for an apology. If readers feel that this could be a helpful step, Nicole urges them to do so.

There is a deep intrinsic value in expressing how we feel and how we view the past. However, we must keep in mind that often parent figures are not as open to these conversations. Decades of learned behavior do not just evaporate when you point them out. It's important to allow the anger in and communicate it, but it should be done without expecting an outside party to validate our experiences.

Nicole urges readers to spend a few moments exploring which of the four pillars of reparenting they need to work on.

Emotional regulation:
As children, many of us were not taught the value or practice of being emotionally aware. We can begin cultivating emotional regulation by:

- Practicing deep belly breathing
- Witnessing the sensations that different emotions activate in your body
- Noticing what causes you to feel emotionally activated
- Allowing emotional responses without judgment, allowing any and all emotions to pass through you while simply witnessing them.

Loving discipline:
You can cultivate a loving distance by:

- Keeping small promises to yourself each day
- Developing daily rituals and routines
- Saying no to things that do not serve you
- Holding boundaries even when you are uncomfortable doing so
- Disconnecting and spending time in self-reflection
- Clearly stating your needs in objective (nonjudgmental) language

Self-care:
You can cultivate self-care by:

- Going to bed a bit earlier
- Cooking and eating a home-cooked meal
- Meditating for five minutes (or longer)

- Moving your body for five minutes (or longer)
- Journaling
- Spending time in and connecting to nature
- Allowing the sun to touch your skin
- Connecting with someone you love

Childlike wonder:

As adults, it's crucial to remember to play, connect with, and develop hobbies we enjoy. You can cultivate this joy by:

- Dancing or singing freely
- Doing something unplanned
- Finding a new hobby or interest
- Listening to your favorite music
- Complimenting a stranger
- Doing something you loved doing as a child
- Connecting with friends and loved ones

Emotional Maturity

Emotional immaturity is common and revolves around the inability to tolerate. Such people have trouble tolerating their own emotions and cope with anger by slamming a door or by deploying silent treatment. The outcome for children of emotionally immature parent figures is loneliness, emptiness, or being alone in the world. This feeling comes from a continued disconnection from our authentic Self. Those of us raised in homes where free self-expression was not supported may find ourselves overly focused on what others think or feel about us.

We might not like all parts of who we are, yet they exist and must be acknowledged. When our core sense of self is dependent and open to outside influence, even what we think others believe about us can shape the way we see ourselves. When we are authentically ourselves, we will encounter judgment and criticism. One of the major achievements of emotional maturity is learning how to be at peace with being misunderstood.

The Ninety-Second Rule

The fundamental aspect of emotional maturity is the ability to be aware of and regulate our emotions to allow others to express themselves. Emotions usually only last for ninety seconds and come to an end. If left alone, this ninety-second irritation can grow into days of irritability, anger, and years of grudge. However, this physiological event can be stopped in ninety seconds by intervening with our minds. We can use the power of our conscious mind to create another, more positive reality. When we resist the habit of creating a story about where our emotions came from, we shorten our body's often prolonged physiological reactions.

Coping With Emotional Maturity

Emotional maturity allows us the opportunity to choose how to respond to the external world. Instead of instinctually falling back into the coping strategies of our childhood, proactive soothing methods involve making a conscious choice. For Nicole, walking or doing the dishes helps soothe her growing emotions. For others, it may be taking a bath or reading. Another important coping strategy is to increase our ability to tolerate distress. Some of us may have to learn to endure our distress. Enduring requires an inner trust that soothing methods do not; we have to have faith in ourselves that we will get through this.

If we feel overwhelmed, it is best to take ourselves out of a situation before we feel emotional activation. Permitting ourselves to say 'no' and practicing emotional boundaries can help with soothing too. Nicole urges parents to take care of themselves physically and emotionally to be better parents to their children. Parents who have cultivated emotional maturity can then devote their resources to helping their children deal with emotions.

We must remember that it is okay to be imperfect and extend similar compassion to our parent figures. As we continue to dig more and more to understand their conditioning and life circumstances, we can begin to empathize without explaining the problems. Meditation has been known to help curb emotional activation to a vast degree. Whenever we feel judged or misunderstood, we can learn to look at it as a physiological response that has no reflection on who we are.

Inner Emotional Maturity Beams Outward

When life becomes stressful or after we have had a moment of stress-induced reactivity, it can be helpful to touch base with the events that impacted our experiences. Some questions that can help us get a firm hold on our reactivity before we are taken over by it include:

- What can I learn about myself from what happened?
- What patterns brought me here?
- How can I embrace discomfort and grow from it?
- How can I learn how to accept criticism without making it absolute truth?
- How can I forgive myself and others?

Do the Work: Develop Emotional Maturity and Resilience

Nicole has outlined some guidelines for readers to follow through on their emotional maturity and its development.

Step 1. Reconnect with and rediscover your emotions.
To develop the ability to identify your feelings, you will first want to get more connected with how your body responds to emotional events. Body connection meditation can help with the process. By meditating and focusing on how we're feeling, we can begin to reconnect with our bodies and our emotions.

Step 2. Help your body return to balance.
Here are some soothing techniques that can help restore emotional balance:
- Taking a bath
- Self-massage
- Reading
- Listening to, playing, or writing music.
- Expressing your emotions
- Writing
- Engaging in breathwork.
- Spending time outside in nature.
- Meditating or praying.

Here are some prompts that one can use as daily affirmations in their journals:

- Today I am practicing being conscious of my body's changing emotional state.
- I am grateful for an opportunity to work on becoming more emotionally mature.
- Today, I am able to connect with my body to help me understand my emotions.
- Change in this area allows me to feel more connected to my emotional world.
- Today I am practicing when I take moments throughout my day to check in with my body's sensations.

Interdependence

Nicole expounds that the task of emotional maturity is an everyday process. As we change our mind and brain and access our authentic Self, we create joy, creativity, empathy, acceptance, collaboration, and eventually oneness with our greater community. This is interdependence, a state of authenticity and connectedness that is the ultimate testament to the power of holistic healing. We find the divine in ourselves, which extends to the world around us.

Finding the Self-Healer Community

Nicole started The Holistic Psychologist in 2018, looking for people to share her experiences with. The word spread and another intention emerged: to build a safe and secure community that would foster the greatest possible space for healing.

Connection is inherent in the human condition. Loneliness increases the rates of autoimmune diseases and chronic illnesses in many of the same ways that trauma does. Ambivalent relationships have detrimental effects on our mental and physical health as well. Half of all married couples view their spouses ambivalently. Such relationships are often trauma bonds and not based on authenticity.

Interdependence is the act of being separated together. Once we've expressed our needs and openly established our boundaries, we can enter an arena where we feel secure. When we have trust in our inner world, knowing that we have the tools to face the assorted trials that life will bring, we can reflect that trust and security out into our community. When we've connected to our authenticity, we can start to recognize the people who belong in our lives. The soul flutters to let us know that we were meant to cross paths with this human.

Over time, we can learn how to define ourselves in relation to others and return to our authentic Self. Many of us are afraid of being vulnerable and the interconnectedness of humans. However, when we peel back the layers of our psyche, we can appreciate our similarities with the people we love and the community we live in. We can participate in this expression of collective unity only when we are calm and balanced. Those around us often mirror our internal state; when we feel safe, others feel safe, too. We have to remember that we're not alone in our struggle.

When we feel safe and secure, we feel comfortable enough to express our internal state. Those who never fight or disagree are locked in a dysregulated system that is artificially hampering their stress. Achieving intimacy requires expressing our authentic selves without fear of being misunderstood. All of us deserve to have the opportunity to return to a safe home.

By breaking down these barriers between us as individuals, we can become receptive to connecting with things that transcend our human comprehension. Chief Black Elk of the Oglala Sioux Nation said, "The first peace, which is most important, is that which comes from the souls of people when they realize their relationship, their oneness, with the universe and all its powers, and when they realize that at the center of the universe dwells the Great Spirit and that this center is really everywhere, it is within each of us."

As we heal ourselves, we heal the world around us.

Do The Work: Assess Your Interdependent Relationships

Nicole urges readers to assess their interdependence by asking the following questions:

- Are you comfortable establishing and maintaining clear boundaries in all relationships?
- Can you hold space for open communication and for emotional processing for yourself and others?
- Do you feel free to speak your truth and reality even when they don't align with those of others? Are you clear about your intentions when you act?
- Can you witness your ego without acting on every thought?

FSJ: Creating Interdependence

We can start to cultivate interdependence by determining the areas we need to strengthen and making new choices. The following prompts can help:

- Today, I am practicing creating interdependence in my relationships.
- I am grateful for an opportunity to create more fulfilling relationships.
- Today, I am able to express myself authentically and still feel connected to others.
- Change in this area allows me to feel connected to my authentic self and needs in all relationships.
- Today I am practicing when I speak my truth to my partner about how I felt about our recent argument.

Goal:

In the third part of How to do the work by Dr. Nicole Lepera, the author shows readers how they can use the knowledge they've gained from the first two parts and apply it in their real lives to manifest real change. Awakening is a rebirth of the self that involves tearing down parts of who we were when we lived in an autopilot state of existence. This part of the book teaches readers how to reparent themselves. We begin by learning how to identify our physical, emotional, and spiritual needs, and then we practice noticing the conditioned way we've gone about attempting to get those needs met. As we change our mind and brain and access our authentic Self, we create joy, creativity, empathy, acceptance, collaboration, and eventually oneness with our greater community.

Lesson:

Activity 1:
There are four pillars to consider while reparenting ourselves. Can you cope with stress flexibly and adaptively? Can you keep small promises and develop daily routines and habits? Do you have time for self-care? Are you working towards rediscovering your childlike sense of wonder?

Activity 2:
The fundamental aspect of emotional maturity is being aware of and regulating our emotions to allow others to express themselves. How do you respond to the external world? Are you okay with being misunderstood in your journey towards emotional maturity? Can you permit yourself to say 'no' and

practice emotional boundaries to manage your mental space?

Activity 3:
Interdependence is the act of being your authentic self while being in a relationship with others. Are you comfortable establishing and maintaining clear boundaries in all relationships? Can you hold space for open communication and emotional processing for yourself and others? Do you feel free to speak your truth and reality even when they don't align with others? Are you clear about your intentions when you act?

Checklist:

Key takeaways from Part 1 are:
- With the help of the wise inner parent, we can learn how to validate our reality and feelings by witnessing them rather than instinctually judging or ignoring them.
- Instead of instinctually falling back into the emotional coping strategies of our childhood, it is best to consciously choose proactive soothing methods such as taking a bath or a walk.
- By meditating and focusing on how we're feeling, we can begin to reconnect with our bodies and our emotions.
- Interdependence is the act of being separated together wherein we express our needs and openly establish our boundaries.

Action Plan:

- Practice the art of self-awareness by allowing emotional

responses without judgment and simply witnessing them through the eyes of a third person.

- Reconnect with your emotions through meditation and help your body return to balance with soothing techniques such as reading, taking a bath, or engaging in breathwork.
- Cultivate interdependence by determining the areas in which you need to strengthen and make new choices.

Conclusion

These summaries have only shown a small portion of 'How to Do the Work.' We have elucidated the fundamentals of the book, but there has been much skipped over. Some of Dr. Nicole LePera's personal experiences and her anecdotes about her clients have been excluded in this summary. However, the core teachings of the book, including the 'Do the work' section and the 'Future Self Journal Prompts,' have been added to give readers a guideline to work with.

Every moment, we have a choice to live in the past or envision a future that is different from our current state. Most of us are unable to take a leap of faith and work on our SelfHealing since our mind craves the familiar. The purpose of this book is to let readers know that there is another door they can choose to take. The art of healing is a long road, and Dr. LePera makes a conscious effort to work on SelfHealing every day. She urges readers to reflect on their past, identify their egos, and bring forth the authentic self lying underneath the pile of years of emotional regression.

Thank You!

Hope you've enjoyed your reading experience.

We here at Life Lessons will always strive to deliver to you the highest quality guides.

So, I'd like to thank you for supporting us and reading until the very end.

Before you go, would you mind leaving us a review on Amazon?

It will mean a lot to us and support us in creating high-quality guides for you in the future.

Thanks once again, and here's where you can leave a review.

Warmly yours,

The **Life Lesson** Team

Manufactured by Amazon.ca
Bolton, ON

22331420R00052